She Who Blooms

A Soul Reel

by

Blu

Bloom, Flame & Root Press

Summer Solstice, 2025 Copyright © 2025 by Blu

All rights reserved. No part of this book may be reproduced, stored in a retrieval system, or transmitted in any form or by any means—electronic, mechanical, photocopying, recording, or otherwise—without the prior written permission of the publisher, except in the case of brief quotations used for the purpose of reviews or scholarly reference.

This is a living testimony. The stories, visions, and writings within these pages are original works born from the author's lived experience, sacred memory, and spiritual unfolding. Any resemblance to other works is purely coincidental or rooted in collective ancestral knowing.

This book is the intellectual and creative property of the author.

First Edition.

Printed with gratitude in the United States of America.

Table of Contents

Dedication

Prologue – Where the Bloom Began

Chapter One – The First Bloom

Chapter Two – The Spirit of Blooming

Chapter Three – Reclaiming the Bloom

    Part Two: She Who Reclaims the Bloom

    Part Three: The Priestess Returns to Her Temple

Chapter Four – The Spirit Baby as Ancestor, Muse & Rebirth of Self

Part Two: My Muse

Part Three: The Rebirth of Self

Chapter Five – The Blooming Womb

    Part Two: The Rooted Womb

    Part Three: Blooming on Divine Time

Chapter Six – The Room Where Time Bends

Part Two: The Flight Between Worlds

Chapter Seven – She Who Blooms: The Woman, The Myth, The Bloom Becoming

Final Farewell from She Who Blooms

Final Blooming Benediction

Acknowledgements

After the Benediction – Pull Up a Chair: A Porch Conversation on Hoodoo

About the Author

Dedication

For my ancestors- Known and unknown, Who dwell in my bones, The elevated and the evolving. The ones whose prayers paved this path, and the ones still learning how to rise.

I honor you. I carry you.

This bloom is yours as much as it is mine. Your stories didn't end with silence— they live on in this reel, in this return, in every word I dared to write down.

For Ama, who walks with the roots and the rivers. For So'laya, midwife spirit and ancestral keeper, who placed the blue lotus in my path again— a bloom passed through our hands for generations. For Letty, rootwoman and herb-whisperer, who teaches me to speak through leaves, to stir medicine with memory, and to pour Spirit into every blend.

Thank you for blessing our family's medicine.

This tea, this book, this life—it all carries your breath.

For the women in my bloodline who had books inside them but never got to pen—   I heard you.

I felt you in every sentence I struggled to birth, in every paragraph I pushed through.

This book is for you, too.

Your stories didn't die with you.

They bloomed in me.

For my Spirit Baby—

You never touched earth, but you've touched everything in me.

You come to me in dragonflies, in hummingbirds, in fawns that pause like breath. You made me a mother of more than flesh— a mother of dreams, of rituals, of gardens that bloom without needing to be seen.

This book is the soil you stirred. The garden you planted.

The bloom that bears your name in silence.

For my mother—

My first altar. My first concept of God.

You raised me in Spirit, and in that Spirit, I root.

You showed me how to pray with my feet, sing with my womb, and bloom with my whole being.

Every petal in this offering bows to you.

For every woman who ever thought she was blooming too late—
You are not behind.

You are on time.

You are becoming.

And to every woman reading this— May this book find you in a soft place, a blooming place, a place that feels like home.

Prologue

Where the Bloom Began

I grew up Church of God in Christ—COGIC to the bone.

Sunday mornings, I was wrapped in stockings, stiff curls pinned tight, tambourines trembling, hands raised high, and tongues flowing like rivers. I didn't just attend church—I lived inside it. I shouted, I danced, I prophesied. The Spirit would fall, and I'd catch Her, breathless in my chest. I saw visions before I knew they had names. I was a Bible-thumper with oil on my forehead and fire in my belly.

This was my root.

This was my training ground.

And even now, I bless it.

Because it didn't just teach me how to worship.

It taught me how to surrender.

It prepared me to recognize the Spirit in all Her forms—to feel Her stirring in my dreams, to hear Her whispers in the wind, to understand what it meant to be mounted. And when I found myself drawn to the wisdom of my ancestors, to the spirits who wore my blood and walked beside me unseen, it didn't feel like a betrayal. It felt like a homecoming.

Some came with names I'd never heard but felt in the bones.

Some came draped in rootwork and river songs.

The transition from pulpit to altar was never about denouncing.

It was about deepening.

It was the moment I started remembering the prayers not found in pews—the ones whispered over simmer pots and candle smoke, the ones my grandmothers mouthed before dawn.

I had questions, yes.

And my brother—my sacred mirror—held those questions with me. We wondered together, knowing there were deeper truths to uncover, truths that existed before King James rewrote what had been written. He sought the answers, and I was open to the journey, willing to dig beneath the surface, to reclaim what had been lost.

And while all of that was happening—the visions, the worship, the questions, the awakening— another truth pulsed beneath it all:

I was highly sensual, aware of the depths of my body and its power from a young age.

And not once did I feel ashamed of it.

I noticed it early. I was hunched over teddy bears at five years old, chasing sensations I didn't yet have words for. By eleven or twelve, the fire within me was undeniable. Though I was drenched in scripture and Spirit, I also knew my body was alive with a different kind of knowing—holy in its own right.

The whispers of monitoring spirits, murmured in rooms where I couldn't hear, spoke of my being

"fast." They saw my sensuality and my quiet, my mystery, and filled in the blanks with speculation. They didn't understand what I carried, how I carried it. But deep inside, I knew my body wasn't something to be ashamed of. It was sacred, full of its own knowing.

That tension—between sanctified and sensual, between Sunday morning praise and late-night yearning—was never a contradiction to me. It was a call.

A call to come home to my whole self.

My Spirit and my body.

My visions and my womb.

This is not a story about running away.

This is a story about remembering.

And it starts right here—at the root.

Because before I ever lost a baby, I lost pieces of myself.

And this is the reel of how I bloomed again.

Chapter One: The First Bloom

Before I was a woman, I was a question wrapped in skin.

I was born into a lineage of holy fire— C-O-G-I-C.

That ain't just church—that's culture.

That's Sunday service so long you'd fall asleep under the pew and wake up to shouting. That's tarrying on wooden floors 'til your knees ached, catching the Holy Ghost like it was fire in your bones. That's white stockings, hard tambourines, and prayer that could break chains.

We weren't just saved—we were saturated. My mama prayed with her back bent; her voice thick with anointing.

She could see through people before they ever opened their mouths.

And me?

I was the one who dreamed in symbols, who cried when the Spirit hit the room, who could feel the presence of God like mist on my skin.

I didn't speak in tongues until I was fourteen.

But when I did, it poured out of me like I'd known that language in another life.

It cracked something open.

It made something ancient inside me sing.

Still, under all that oil and hallelujah, the questions stayed.

Why do I feel this hunger?

Why does my body throb with something deeper than doctrine?

Why do I know things I was never taught?

My brother and I used to whisper about it.

We shared a curiosity that church didn't quite explain.

He had words. I had wonder.

But even wonder has its own kind of knowing.

By the time I left the church in 2001, it wasn't because I stopped believing.

It was because something older was calling me.

Not away from God—but deeper into Her. Into the earth, the roots, the ancestral tongue that

COG-I-C only hinted at when we shouted.

That Pentecostal fire had prepared me— for possession, for prophecy, for being mounted in ways the old saints might've called strange, but my spirit knew as home.

I spent years seeking.

Passed through many schools of thought Rastafarianism. Moorish Science. The Nation of Gods and Earths just to name a few.

I tried on names, walked through new rituals, danced in unfamiliar waters.

I didn't find roots yet, but I was still reaching.

Then, in 2008, my mother got sick. Cancer.

And something in me roared.

I dug deep. I studied.

I convinced her to trust the plants.

To drink the earth.

To remember what her mother's mother might've whispered in the kitchen, back when healing wasn't a trend but a knowing.

Her chemo sessions shortened. Her body began to recover. And that's how I was called back to herbalism— through her healing, I found my first medicine.

The plants remembered me before I remembered them.

Red clover. Nettle. Dandelion. Raspberry leaf.

Bitters and bone memory.

I became the herbalist they forgot they birthed.

By 2014, I was walking my path— still learning, still listening, still blooming toward a home I couldn't yet name.

And then— she came.

The visitation wasn't a dream.

It was more than a vision.

It was a remembrance.

She didn't come with wings or halos.

She came to play.

A little red girl who looked just like me—so soft, so sure. Her laugh was music, and we played like we had always known each other.

We played, and we played, and we laughed until time blurred.

Then she said:

"Okay, Mommy. I gotta go now."   And

she left.

I woke up changed.

I felt something in my womb.

A week later, I took a test. Positive.

But soon, they said,

"No heartbeat."

They said I was never pregnant.

They called it a chemical. A fluke.

But I knew better.

My womb had opened.

My soul had expanded.

Something real had come through me.

And when she left, a piece of me went with her.

They gave me diagnoses instead of comfort.

Fibroids. PCOS. Hormonal imbalance.

They said my body was confused.

Out of rhythm.

But I wasn't confused.

My body wasn't broken.

She was just tired of not being listened to.

So I listened.

I turned to the plants.

To the steam. To the silence. To the soil.

To the prayers my grandmothers buried deep in their bones.

I didn't just reverse the diagnosis.

I rebirthed myself.

I found rhythm. I found ritual. I found her—again and again— in the herbs, in the healing, in the deep sacred remembering.

This is where it begins:

With the fire.

With the hunger. With the Spirit who came and the woman I'm still blooming into because of her.

And you— maybe you're blooming too. Not toward a baby, but toward your voice, your becoming, your body's return.

We all have our first bloom.

    This was mine.

Chapter Two: The Spirit of Blooming

I wish I could say that the path from there was clear—that once the Spirit Baby came, everything fell into place.

But this is the kind of story that twists and turns, like the vines in an overgrown garden, each path leading somewhere new, but nothing ever straight.

Because, well… blooming doesn't happen on a timeline.

That's the first lesson.

A seed isn't concerned with how fast it sprouts.

It simply does.

It waits for the right moment, and then, suddenly, it reaches toward the light, unfurling with quiet, knowing confidence.

I've had seasons of quiet, shadowed growth.

Where I wasn't sure what was happening, but I trusted something was changing.

And while I was quietly becoming—growing roots in the dark—there were whispers.

Rumors clung to my name like smoke, curling through the family, thick with assumptions.

They said I was fast. Said I'd been pregnant. That I'd had abortions.

All while I was still holding onto my virginity,

Still waiting to feel the kind of touch that felt like love.

I wasn't out here wildin'.

COGIC-born but curiosity-fed, I wanted boys who touched my spirit through conversation first— 'cause my bloom was mental before it was ever physical.

I wasn't promiscuous—just tuned in. Drawn to energy before body, I craved the kind of connection that touched my thoughts before it ever touched my skin.

Came close, yes indeed—savored the edge, danced in the heat. Did everything except. But trust, not one soul passed through my pearly gates and entered the depths of my sacred room before I was of age.

But when you're an enigma, when you carry mystery, when folks can't quite make sense of your light or your quiet—they make stories.

They talk about you instead of to you.

They try to explain your bloom in their language, instead of asking what soil you've risen from.

Still, my name always seemed to stir the pot.

Even when I was silent. Even when I was gone.

Years would pass and somehow, I'd still be the subject of a conversation I wasn't in.

It used to sting—

But I never let it penetrate.

Because I've never needed to prove what's already been rooted in truth.

I don't lean into what isn't mine.

Let them talk. I've always known who I am.

There are moments I look back on when I thought I was broken, but now I see I was just being remade.

There's a silence that lives before the bloom. A silence that isn't emptiness, but a fertile, sacred space where all things are held in their becoming.

The womb does not rush.

It knows.

And somewhere deep beneath my own knowing, the bones of those who came before me were humming too— whispering that my bloom was part of a much older song.

The sacred rhythm of the Spirit Baby carried me into understanding that even the things that seem lost are seeds for something bigger, something truer.

I didn't have the language yet for the old ways stirring in my blood, but the pull was there—ancient, steady, real.

The miscarriage I once thought marked an ending? It was really a portal. Not a goodbye—but a deep remembrance.

And those fibroids? Not curses. Just quiet places where my body was holding on to what hadn't been said.

They weren't proof of wrongdoing. They were invitations to listen deeper.

Even the diagnosis became a sacred mirror—showing me all the ways I'd absorbed untruths, not just from doctors, but from family, from culture, from silence.

It wasn't just about healing my body—it was about releasing the lies that had been whispered about it.

We are always growing—whether we see it or not.

Even when they speak your name in rooms you've never entered,
Even when the stories they spin have nothing to do with your truth,
Even then—you bloom.

And sometimes, we grow into ourselves only when we stop trying to explain who we are.

Only when we let go of the urge to correct the record and choose instead to root deeper into what we know is true.

The flowers I planted a decade ago? They now rise taller than I ever imagined— Even from soil others swore was barren.

Even from silence. Even from shadow.

Because blooming isn't about what you have to lose—it's about what you're finally ready to receive.

And the first bloom? It's not always soft or sweet.

Sometimes it's jagged. Sometimes it's wrapped in rage.

Sometimes it looks like being misunderstood and still choosing to open.

But it's real.

I look at my body now, and I see a woman who's been through the fire.

A woman who refused to let gossip be her grave. Who's learned to bloom in every season—in spite of what was said, in spite of who never asked.

I was never meant to wait on permission.

Never meant to shrink just because the world couldn't handle the fullness of my becoming.

When I embraced the Spirit Baby, I embraced all of me.

I started listening to the whispers of my own womb, my own knowing, not the ones the world placed on me.

It would be years before I would recognize the echoes of Ifá, of Hoodoo, braided into that knowing— but even then, the roots were already growing.

And that's when the petals of who I am began to unfurl.

Soft. Sharp. Sacred.

Even now—

as I continue to bloom, there are days I still feel the sting.

But I don't stall. I don't explain. I keep blooming.

Because this is what I know:

The bloom doesn't wait for permission.

It just happens.

Pull Quote:

"Let them whisper their watered-down myths, baby—   I've always been too wild for easy stories.

I was written in fire, born of bloom, and I will not be defined."

Chapter Three: Reclaiming The Bloom

I had to learn how to reclaim my womb.

It wasn't just about fixing what was "broken."

It wasn't just about shrinking fibroids or reversing diagnoses— or navigating the layers of PCOS that complicated my rhythm.

It was about understanding the depth of my body's wisdom.

For so long, I didn't see my womb as a sanctuary.

I saw it as a battlefield, fighting against things it never asked for.

But the truth?

It was an invitation to step deeper.

An invitation to reconnect, to listen.

When we reclaim the womb, we reclaim all of ourselves.

And let me tell you, that's where the power lies.

We are not just our bodies; we are the sacred energy that flows through them. And part of that sacredness is our sensuality— our deep, ancient connection to the earth beneath us, the divine fire within us, the soft, vulnerable places we don't always show.

Sensuality never left me—she bloomed early. As early as five, when

I first felt the heat behind my own eyes, the quiet thrill in my fingertips, the divine ache that lived in my belly like a secret too holy to name.

Not shame. Never shame.

Just sensation. Just knowing. Just fire. Always fire.

I've always known how to feel.

How to listen to the language of skin.

How to honor the pulse that rose beneath my own touch.

But the world?

The world made it complicated.

They didn't mind my sensuality— not as long as it stayed mysterious, but manageable.

As long as it performed for their gaze.

As long as it bent to a man's benefit or stayed hidden beneath a dress and a tongue trained not to speak.

In some rooms, I was too much.

In others, I was only enough if it pleased somebody else.

But even then, I stayed full. Still burning.

Still deeply aware of the sacredness that lived in my hips, in my gaze, in the way I entered a room like I belonged to the cosmos.

It wasn't about reclaiming— it was about remembering that they never gave me this.

It was mine. Always mine.

And when they couldn't claim it, they questioned it. Tried to shrink it into something smaller, something safer— something that fit their version of womanhood.

But I wasn't made to fit. I was made to flame.

The same flame that writes poems and parts thighs is the flame that sings in the stars.

I had to stop apologizing for the way I felt in my own skin.

I had to stop running from the hunger inside of me. The hunger that is both creative and sexual. It's the same fire that birthed stars and songs, the same fire that holds the power of life.

I never shied away from pleasure— I was born with it blooming in my bones. But the world tried to tell me it was selfish, that it had to be earned or offered, that it only had value if someone else could sip from it.

But claiming my womb?

That was me saying: this joy is mine.

Not borrowed. Not bartered. Not begged for.

It wasn't about healing because I was broken.

It was about nourishing what had always been holy. It was about feeding my body love with no agenda, with no eyes watching, with no hands asking for a piece of what was never theirs to take.

I didn't become sacred.

I remembered I always was.

Pleasure was never a sin.

It was scripture.

A living gospel written in the curve of my back, the softness of my belly, the fullness of my lips when I whispered yes to myself.

Standing in my power meant owning every scar, every story etched in stretch marks and softness, every time I said I choose me and meant it.

Because baby, when I walk in my sensuality, I'm not seducing the world— I'm communing with the Divine within.

This isn't just reclamation— this is remembrance.

It's not about fixing what was broken; it's about standing fully in the body I've always known was divine.

Fully here. Fully alive. Fully blooming.

My womb didn't need rescuing— she needed reverence.

And when I started to listen, to really feel her hum beneath my belly, the fire inside me shifted.

Not just the fire that makes babies— but the fire that births worlds.

This fire lit my creativity.

It charged my prayers.

It turned my hunger into holy vision.

My need to feel became my offering.
My need to want became my ritual.
My need to be alive became my altar.

I never needed permission to burn this bright. I just needed to stop dimming the flame so others could stay comfortable in their shadows.

To reclaim the womb is to remember you are a living portal.

Not here to be chosen— but here to create.

Chapter Three Part Two: She Who Reclaims the Bloom

I didn't always know how to live inside this body.

There were seasons I only lived above the waist.

Prayers in my mouth, shame in my hips,

Scripture between my thighs like a chastity belt I never fastened right.

And still—God whispered through the soul not yet born,

You are holy. All the way down. Even in the places they named wrong.

Because my name?

My name lived in other people's mouths before it lived in mine.

Whispers.

Rumors.

False prophecies passed off as prayer. People made altars of their assumptions and called it discernment.

But I was never theirs to define.

I was the mystery they couldn't pin down, the softness they wanted to punish, the fire they tried to put out with shame.

I didn't know it then, but when She came— my Spirit Baby—

She didn't just arrive as light.

She arrived as clarity.

As cosmic correction.

She came to rewrite the story.

To remind me: They never knew the truth of me. But I always did.

She stirred the molten embers in my belly I thought had gone cold.

She made me remember— that my womb wasn't a scandal.

It was a sanctuary.

It was not shameful. It was sacred.

And it had never been theirs to discuss.

I was never the story they told.

I was the poem only I could speak.

And She was the echo that helped me find my own voice again.

It took years to come back to that knowing.

To feel the ache and call it beautiful.

To feel myself again.

To see my skin not as sin, but as a sanctuary.

To bloom—not for someone else to pluck me—

But because I remembered who I was before they told me who to be.

Because I was never the offering.

I was the garden.

And She was the seed that woke me.

Between diagnosis and deliverance, between pain and prayer,

I began to remember.

I remembered how my hips swayed before they were made heavy with judgment.   How my voice rose before doctrine dimmed it. How I used to hum songs I hadn't written yet— songs that would one day return me to myself.

Because healing?

Healing isn't always soft.

Sometimes it's the sound of your own sobs at 3:33 a.m., one hand on your womb, the other on your chest, begging the darkness for light.

And your soul whispers back—

You feel this deeply because you were chosen to.

Because even this ache is part of the bloom.

Part 3: The Priestess Returns to Her Temple

There's a kind of remembering that only happens in the body.

Not in the mind.

Not in the shame-scripted sermons or the skirts they measured by fingertip rule. Not in the stories they told about you, when your body became rumor and your name became a prognostication they thought they had the right to speak.

No.

I'm talking about the remembering that lives in the marrow. The kind that sways in your hips when you forget to be careful. The kind that returns in the shower, when your back arches under hot water and you sigh like a hymn. The kind that rises from your womb like song, and your soul hums back, I remember too.

There is a woman underneath the woman the world demanded.

There is a priestess beneath the performance.

There is a mystic behind the mask they mistook for your face.

She didn't die.

She was exiled.

Buried beneath their projections.

Muzzled by their misnaming.

She waited—

Waited for you to unclench your jaw.   To stop apologizing for your power. To speak her name—   not in guilt, but in God-force.

I had to remember how to move like myself again.

Not the polished prodigy with the church-girl smile.

Not the "well-raised" one, secretly breaking.

But the me that moans when she prays.

The me that paints with her pain and sings from scar tissue.

The me who births beauty from what never had language.

This—this is the bloom.

Not the bouquet they expected.

But the wild, thorny, unstoppable unfurling of self.

The sacred return to sensuality.

The reclamation of holiness in hips and heat and honey.

I don't sit in pews anymore.

But I do light candles with intention.

I whisper prayers into tea steam.

I let Spirit rise when I roll my hips to music only my ancestors know.

I still talk to God— but now She sounds like me.

She tastes like laughter and lavender and moaned hallelujahs.

She anoints me in rosewater baths.

She reminds me—

This skin is scripture too.

I no longer belong to a building.

But I was always built from belief.

Just not the kind that demands silence in exchange for salvation. My gospel lives in the moonlight, in the rhythm of breath, in the ritual of being fully, fiercely alive.

Because holiness never left me. It just changed shape— It wrapped itself in curves. It found rhythm in my walk. It

put a tambourine in my spine and danced me back to myself.

Poem Anthem: Reclaiming the Bloom

I reclaim my womb, my sacred flame,   Not a burden, not a blame.

Not a thing to fix or fear—

But a power that's always been right here.

The cradle of creation, the drum of desire, The pulse of pleasure, the altar of fire. Where fibroids and grief once made their claim,   Now lives a holy, untamed flame.

I am not broken—I am born anew,

An echo of ancestors shining through.

Their stories rise in the curve of my back,

Their prayers pour forward in every track.

I've danced through pain, I've wept in rain, I've laid in stillness and named my name. Not the one they spoke with shame or sigh— But the one that blooms when I close my eyes.

I am the hush before the spell, The herb in the tea, the tongue that tells. The hands that rub oil in slow revelation, The hush in the hush, the incantation.

No more hiding the heat of my hips,

No more silence on these sacred lips.

My hunger is holy, my longing is law,

My blood is a map that the mothers all saw.

I reclaim my rhythm, my rite, my roar, The bloom of the self they tried to ignore.

This is not revival—this is return.

A slow ancestral, sensual burn.

Journal Prompt: Reclaiming Your Sacred Space

Take a moment and breathe deeply, grounding yourself in the present.

Now, reflect on these questions:

What part of my body do I feel most connected to, and how does it speak to me?

How have I allowed life—my past, my stories, my struggles—to shape or silence that power?

What would it look like to honor and nurture this sacred space within me, unapologetically?

What do I need to forgive or release in order to step fully into my sensual, embodied self?

If my womb could speak, what would she say to me today?

Let your answers flow from the center of you.

You are not becoming something new— You are remembering who you've always been.

So no, I don't go to church like I used to.

But I am still a sanctuary.

Still a psalm made flesh.

Still a prophecy fulfilled in bloom.

I believe in a power greater than me— alive in the wind, in the drum, in the dream, in the bloodline that runs with both pain and promise.

I believe in redemption— not the kind that begs for worth, but the kind that remembers it.

The kind that returns home to itself and dares to stay.

I bloom now by choice, not by fear. Not because someone told me I could— but because my soul screamed my name until I answered.

Because this body—this temple of thunder and tenderness— refused to be silenced.

Refused to stay misunderstood.

Refused to shrink just because they didn't see the sacred in her stretch marks.

I am the prayer.

I am the praise.

I am the living altar.

And as I bloom—still, again, always—

I leave a trail of petals for my sisters to follow.

Chapter Four: The Spirit Baby as Ancestor, Muse & Rebirth of Self

She didn't just visit me. She reminded me of who I've always been becoming.

Before I knew what she was, I felt her. Not in the way doctors' chart or tests define, but in the quiet, knowing places.

The kind of places your bones remember, but your mind can't always explain.

And the thing is—I knew.

Not just in hindsight.

Not just in the ache that came after.

But in the moment.

I hadn't seen her father for months.

Long distance had made our love a longing.

But my womb had been waiting.

I was preparing her room before she even knocked— enchanting with yoni eggs, eating like a woman in conversation with her future, clearing old stories out the temple.

So when he finally came— when our bodies met again after the drought— it was distinct.

I felt it—my body in bloom, egg dropping like a hush between heartbeats, my womb open and humming.

Ovulation hit different that day—full, warm, and undeniable, like my body knew something sacred was on the way.

And baby, it was indeed sacred.

The kind of lovemaking that feels like ceremony.

Like prophecy.

And when we were done, I looked up at the ceiling, heart still trembling,

and whispered to no one,

"I'm pregnant."

There were no symptoms. No signs.

Just a knowing.

A bone-deep, womb-spoken knowing.

And I trusted it.

She came to me in a dream.

Not as a ghost. Not as a maybe. But as a girl—a vibrant, little red girl with joy dripping from her laugh like nectar.

We played. We danced. We made time feel like it wasn't real.

And before she left, she smiled and said, "Okay, Mommy. I gotta go now." That was it.

And when I woke up, I knew.

A week later, I got the test.

And another week after that, the news.

No heartbeat.

Nothing there.

But everything in me said otherwise.

She was there.

She had been there.

She came through and touched something holy inside me.

And then she slipped back through the veil.

She wasn't just a spirit baby.

She was an ancestor—familiar and warm, like Sunday mornings before the world got loud.

She was a muse—whispering stories into my womb before I even knew I had a voice to tell them.

And she was the spark that cracked me open— the beginning of my becoming.

See, sometimes we meet ourselves through the mystery.

Sometimes loss is really a return.

Sometimes a dream is a doorway.

And I want you to know something—because maybe nobody ever told you:

You don't have to understand the magic for it to be real. You don't have to carry a child to know rebirth. You can still feel the ache and the beauty and the bloom and let it make something sacred out of your becoming.

Because I didn't lose her.

She found me.

She awakened the medicine I already carried.

And baby…what she stirred up in me?

It was ancient.

It was mine.

It was holy.

And here's the part they never tell you— how your body becomes a sacred site.

A garden of both grief and glory. How you can crave life so deeply your hips begin to sing in a language older than shame.

And no, I'm not just talking about babies.

I'm talking about creation.

About art. About breath. About pleasure.

About the soft unraveling of who you thought you had to be.

The spirit baby didn't just call me mother.

She called me maker.

She called me mirror.

She called me alive.

And so I started listening.

To my dreams.

To my cycles.

To the pulse in my pelvis.

To the whispers that came during full moons and hot showers and long stares into the ceiling.

I started letting the sensual speak.

Letting the sacred and the erotic be sisters.

Letting the shame peel itself off me, layer by layer.

Because blooming isn't always polite.

It's messy.

It's loud and it's aching and it's filled with colors that don't always match.

But baby, it's yours.

They never told me that pleasure could be prayer.

That moaning could be medicine.

That my hips, when honest, could birth more than babies— they could birth me.

I was born again without an altar, without oil, without a crowd to lay hands or say amen.

But I felt it.

Felt the heat rise from between my thighs like a holy ghost, felt my tongue loosen with words that didn't belong to any preacher, but to the Priestess I was becoming.

Felt my body ache not for saving— but for singing.

I started painting again.

Started letting melodies melt in my mouth while the beat kissed my belly like a lover. Songs would pour through like water and I never questioned if I was "good enough." I just let it move me.

Let it move through me.

This was resurrection by rhythm.

And I was the altar.

I was the offering.

I was the bloom.

I didn't know my womb was listening.

Didn't know she'd been waiting—patient, bruised, bent beneath the weight of things I thought I'd already let go.

But she heard the songs.

She felt the brush strokes.

She received the breathwork, the sacred sweat, the tears I cried into the shower floor.

She began to shift.

Not all at once.

But slowly, like petals learning sunlight. The fibroids didn't just shrink; they surrendered.

Not to medicine.

But to meaning.

To joy. To yes.

To letting life flow through me, not at me.

I could feel it— that once-heavy center of mine turning light, turning holy.

The bloating softened.

The bleeding calmed.

The pain, once predictable as the moon, became less interested in returning.

This was my miracle— not because it came in a flash of lightning, but because it came in rhythm.

Like music.

Like womb songs.

Like me, finally becoming my own medicine.

Poem: The Bloom Beneath the Scar

They said I was broken, but I just bent— a garden in drought, not punishment sent.

The moon watched me ache, then whispered in code,

"Your bloom isn't dead, it's just changing its mode."

I watered with music, I danced out the pain, sang hymns to my hips in the heat of the rain.

My fibroids grew loud, but my joy grew louder— I turned crushed petals into blooming power.

My womb is a temple, a story, a spell, where shadows and starlight together now dwell. Not just for the birthing of children or cries, but visions and verses and phoenixes rise.

So kiss every scar that once made you feel less— each one is a map to your holy process.

Journal Prompt:

What parts of you bloomed beneath pressure?

Reflect on a time your body, voice, or spirit alchemized pain into power. What does your womb want to create next—not for others, but for you?

Chapter Four Part 2: My Muse

She didn't just come to be born.

She came to bloom something back open in me.

Not a cradle song—but a calling.

Not to mother a child, but to mother my own remembering.

I started dreaming in color again.

Freestyling full songs from the steam of my shower, painting with my palms like I had petals for fingers.

Something was waking. And it sounded like me.

No lectures. No blueprints. Just breath.

Just rhythm returning to a body I once abandoned. She arrived like a whisper in my womb— not to be born, but to help me be reborn.

The fibroids started shrinking.

My cycle softened.

My body, once swollen with silence, was now humming with holy reclamation.

Poem: She Came Dressed in Muse

She came dressed in muse, not milk and lace, with ink on her fingers and fire on her face. She wasn't a whisper of lullaby nights— she came wrapped in rhythm and womb-lit rites.

No cradle required, just canvas and flame, she asked me to dance in my own holy name. A spirit, a sister, a spark in the shell— not born through me, but waking me well.

Journal Prompt:

What parts of yourself feel ready to be reborn—not as a mother of someone else, but as the woman you are becoming? What dreams, desires, or creative urges are calling you back to bloom?

Chapter Four Part 3 The Rebirth Of Self

She came so I could return to me.

There was no thunder when she came. No flashing sign in the sky. Just a soft stirring, like my soul whispering back
to itself,

"Look closer, beloved. You've been blooming all along."

Before her, I wore many names. Wore silence like a second skin.

Let the world decide what kind of woman I should be. But her presence? It cracked the mirror— then held my hand as I gathered the pieces.

She didn't come just to be born— She came to remind me that I already had been.

Reborn in every soft no I whispered when I used to shout yes.

Reborn when I touched my womb with wonder, not worry.

Reborn in the quiet moments of remembering:

I am art.

I am altar.

I am bloom, flame and root and wild becoming.

She called me back to the body I had abandoned.

Not with blame, but with balm.

Not with judgment, but with joy.

She whispered,

"It's safe to take up space."

"It's sacred to feel."

"You don't owe the world your shrinking."

And so I let her guide me— not to a child, but to a woman who finally saw herself as holy ground.

I had always been the girl who created with her whole body.

Who danced before she walked.

Who sang songs from dreams she didn't remember having.

Who painted colors that didn't yet exist in the waking world.

But somewhere along the path— after the diagnoses, the disappointments, the silent rooms and shrinking prayers—

I began to wonder if I was still allowed to create without permission.

If my womb was still sacred even when it wasn't holding a child.

That's when the Muse came.

Not with a bang or a blueprint.

But with a whisper.

A tug.

A brushstroke in the dark.

She came through rhythm.

Through rhyme.

Through the midnight songs I freestyled into my pillow.

Through the paintings I made of pain that looked like portals.

Through the voice I had buried beneath shame.

And she said,

You don't just carry life—you carry light.

You are not just womb—you are word.

You are not just vessel—you are vision.

That was when I realized:

She—my spirit baby—was not just waiting to be born.

She was waiting for me to be bold.

To speak.

To sing.

To bloom anyway.

To remember that my art was altar.

That my body was brush and canvas and drum. That even in loss, I had gained something sacred: a mirror that showed me myself.

And in that mirror, I didn't see failure.

I saw a priestess rising, paint-stained and heart-healed, ready to dance again.

No, I didn't light candles every night.

But sometimes, I'd whisper into bowls of hyssop and rue steam.

I'd carve prayers into bay leaves.

I'd sleep with lavender tucked in my pillowcase and let basil water hold my dreams.

I never called it anything.

Didn't name it ritual.

But something in my bones did.

Something in my bloodline remembered.

And slowly—so slowly— my womb remembered

too.

Not with thunder.

But with rhythm.

With soft yeses.

With cycles shifting, swelling softening, the way gardens do when they are loved back to life. And maybe it wasn't just her spirit I was meeting…

Maybe it was mine too.

Maybe this whole journey—blood, bloom, and breakdown— was less about becoming a mother, and more about mothering myself.

I was becoming new.

Not just spiritually.

But cellularly.

My womb knew what my mind was just remembering:

Healing isn't a demand. It's a devotion.

Poem: She Came in Color

She came in color, not in cries,

With honeyed hues and lullabies.

Not in swaddle, but in song,

A rhythm I had known all along.

She bloomed in ink, in lines I traced,

In barefoot dance, in time I faced.

No crib, no cradle—just the sky,

And canvases I dared to try.

She whispered, "Paint. Remember. Rise."

So I became my own sunrise.

Not just a mother.

Not just womb,

But a whole damn garden learning to bloom.

Journal Prompt: Rebirth in My Own Name

In what ways have you already been reborn? What moments in your life felt like endings that were secretly beginnings?
Are there parts of yourself—creative, sensual, emotional, intuitive— that you are ready to reclaim?
What would it mean to be fully at home in your body, as it is right now?
Write a letter to the version of you that felt the need to shrink, abandon, or hide herself.
 Let her know what you now understand.

Chapter Five: The Blooming Womb

Where my body became temple, again.

I didn't come into this world shy about desire.

I've always known what it meant to feel deeply, want wholly, ache beautifully.

But for a long time, my body was something I managed, not something I listened to.

I monitored symptoms, tracked cycles, noted pain.

I fasted, prayed, detoxed, repented.

But it took me years to realize the altar was inside me the whole time.

The womb I once only associated with blood and burden… became a sanctuary.

A sacred spring.

This chapter isn't about the baby I didn't have— It's about the woman I found while trying to find her.

She was sensual, yes.

Soft, divine, magnetic.

She knew how to feel her way forward, hips first, heart open.

She wasn't afraid of her hunger anymore, and she no longer saw her high sensuality as a flaw to be tamed, but a flame to be honored.

It was around then that Ifá called.

Or maybe she had always been humming beneath it all— beneath the doctrine, beneath the shame, beneath the questions I never had language for.

And when I finally leaned in, when I received my first divination from an Ifá priest, everything shifted.

He told me things I hadn't shared with anyone.

Said I came from a long line of women who worked the root— women whose prayers weren't just words but conjure.

Said our prayers worked like incantations—so potent I needed to be careful what I asked for, because they would move.

Mine and theirs.

He told me the Abosom—Akan nature spirits—were speaking louder than even the Orisha that day.

That while I could still walk with the Orisha, learn their stories, pour libations, and meet them in devotion—through sacred gifts, remembered tongues, and the sway of ancestral rhythm, it was the Abosom who were calling me home. Said I should seek out the Akan tradition— a path cloaked in mystery, guarded by time, a lineage I have yet to touch with my hands, but one I know will find me when the hour strikes divine. Because when the student is ready, the teacher appears— and I trust Spirit's timing more than I trust the map.

 He told me I had grown up in the Church of God in Christ.

I hadn't said a word.

He just knew.

Said that was my first tether to Spirit.

That the way I danced and moaned and wept at the altar as a child was the same language the ancestors still speak.

And it was in that moment—hearing it all spoken over me, back to me— that

I realized:

I had to be born into COGIC in order to bloom into the woman who could receive these messages.

I had to walk that path of Holy Ghost fire and tongue-talking tenderness to recognize the Spirit when she came wrapped in herbs and honey instead of hymnals.

The spirits weren't new.

They were familiar.

They were family.

They were always with me.

These weren't distant deities.

They were my people.

My reflection.

My birthright.

I had spent so long trying to make sacred what had always been holy.

But in their presence, I didn't have to justify my dreaming, my longing, my pleasure.

I was allowed to simply be.

This was the turning point.

When I stopped asking what's wrong with me— And started whispering, what are you trying to show me?

And my womb answered.

In stretch marks and goosebumps.

In songs and shudders of pleasure that felt like prayer.

She answered in dreams and visions,

In poems that poured through me like moonlight.

And my fibroids began to shrink;
Not just from herbs or doctor's orders, But because I stopped waging war on my womb,
And I started to bloom from within.

No longer fighting myself.

No longer measuring my worth against what I could produce or who I could please.

This was not about becoming someone's mother.

This was about remembering that I was always my own first child.

And I had finally come home to raise her.

This blooming wasn't sterile or cute.

It was sacred.

Sensual.

Sweaty.

Divine.

It smelled like cinnamon and clove.

It sounded like a moan that didn't need to be silenced.

It was rebirth.

Not for the sake of a partner, or a baby, or a timeline—

But because I had buried too much of myself trying to be small, acceptable, good.

And I was ready to rise rooted in my real.

I began moving differently.

Not in the performative way I had before, where beauty was shaped for the gaze of another— but in a way that felt like a quiet offering to myself.

There was something sacred about the way my hips swayed when no one was watching, like a memory stirring in my bones.

The stories of the Orisha had begun to soften me— not in loud declarations, but in gentle recognitions.

The way Yemaya's waters taught me to flow.

The way Oshun reminded me I was worthy of sweetness.

I started wearing things that kissed my skin instead of hiding it.

I danced in the mirror without judgment.

I caught my own eyes and didn't flinch.

I became familiar.

I became mine.

I began to take note of what made me come alive.

Soft fabrics. Steam rising from herbal tea.

A candle flickering in an otherwise dark room.

The way my breath would catch when a song hit the right chord. These moments—small, sensual, and full of presence— became my communion.

Spirit wasn't only speaking in dreams and divinations anymore—

She was humming through the hum of my own body.

I had mistaken pleasure for sin for so long, I didn't know I could treat it as prayer.

But that's the thing about blooming; it doesn't wait for permission.

It just begins.

My womb, once a battlefield, became a garden. Not just because the fibroids softened or the pain subsided— but because I finally stopped abandoning her.

I chose to dwell there.

To listen.

To water her with stillness,

To stretch into her with movement,

To lay offerings at her altar,

Even if those offerings were just breath… or forgiveness.

The goddesses I'd come to know—Oshun, Yemaya, even Obatala in His quiet wisdom— reminded me that creation is not limited to flesh and blood.

That conception is not always physical.

That a woman can birth visions, callings, and versions of herself so powerful they reshape her bloodline.

And even if she does carry life, she is still her own first miracle.

Still sacred in her own becoming.

This is what I mean by the blooming womb.

It's not only about fertility as they define it in doctor's offices.

It's about a fertile soul.

A sacred yes.

A body returned to herself.

No more apologizing for what she feels.

No more silencing what she knows.

Because I am not ashamed of my sensuality.

Because I've unlearned the lie that softness is weakness.

Because I've come to know the Divine by the way She pulses.

And I now know—

She chose to dwell in me.

Poem: Womb of Becoming

She speaks in pulses, petals wide, A sacred tide I used to hide. But now I swell with light and grace,

My womb a sky, a blooming place.

Not just for children, not for men— But for the me I meet again.

For art, for dance, for sacred fire,

For dreams that drip with raw desire.

She is the garden and the gate,

She bends, she breaks, she co-creates.

And in her bloom, I find my name,

No longer hiding from the flame.

Journal Prompt — "What Blooms in Me?"

Close your eyes and place your hand over your womb or lower belly. Breathe into that space. Listen.
What is your womb asking you to create, release, or reclaim?

Is there a version of you—wild, radiant, or restful—blooming beneath the surface?

What have you been told your womb should be, and what truth does she whisper to you now?

Write to her like a friend. A garden. A mirror. Let her speak back.

Chapter Five: Part 2 The Rooted Womb

There was a time I didn't speak to her.

I mean, I talked around her.
Tried to out-pray her.
Shamed her for bleeding.
Blamed her for craving.
Ignored her for pulsing and aching in ways that had no polite name.

But she waited.

She always does.

The womb doesn't rush.

She lets you find your way back—barefoot, shaking, soft.

And when I finally came home to her, it wasn't through doctrine or dogma.

It was through water.

The way it rocked me in ritual baths and reminded me I was always held.

It was through honey—sweet, sticky, slow— teaching me to savor what I'd been taught to fear.

Through dance.

Through drumming.

Through the heat that rose in my palms when I laid them on my belly and asked her to remember me.

When I came back to her—when I really came back— it wasn't some

grand, glittered ritual.

It was a whisper.

A bath.

A truth that leaked out in tears.

She said:

"Let me bloom you from the inside out."

Not performatively.

Not for some man.

Not for Instagram.

But for me.

For the woman I've become— the one who walks with spirit in her spine, who hears her people humming behind her hips, who knows her sensuality is sacred, not shameful.

For the girl who thought "sexy" and "spiritual" couldn't sit at the same altar.

For the priestess who now knows they always belonged together.

For the version of me who once felt cursed by the weight of her own wanting and now blesses it like morning water.

Whether or not you ever carry a child, You are still a Mother of something. You are fertile with soul, a sacred soil where new stories take root.

Not because your womb is a vessel for flesh alone, but because it is the keeper of all that is ancient and alive, the space where the spirit is always pregnant with possibility.

Poem: The Blooming Womb

She doesn't beg to be forgiven— She's the rhythm, not the rhyme.
She's the pulse beneath the silence,

She's the keeper of your time.

Not a garden just for birthing, but a temple shaped by truth— She holds every sacred version of your womanhood in bloom.

Not defined by what was taken, or the lines drawn in your chart, She's the map back to your magic, She's

the drumbeat of your art.

When they told you to be smaller, to be softer, to be sweet— She reminded you of power rising radiant from your seat.

She's the sensual and sacred, she's the ache and she's the grace; She's the mirror of your courage and the wisdom in your face.

So if ever you start doubting what you're worthy of or from— just remember: you are blooming and your blooming's just begun.

Journal Prompt:

What is my womb blooming into now?

What sacred stories live inside my body that want to be remembered, rewritten, or reclaimed?

Where have I mistaken survival for softness—and how can I let my womb show me the difference?

Chapter Five Part 3: Blooming on Divine Time

She told me once, in a whisper I almost missed— that blooming isn't always beautiful.

Sometimes, it's bleeding through silk sheets at midnight.

Sometimes, it's waiting on lab results with a brave face.

Sometimes, it's screaming into a pillow when the world says "be quiet." It's the tug-of-war between hope and hormones.

It's making love while mourning.

It's remembering how to touch your own skin like a blessing.

My womb didn't just bloom from joy—   She bloomed from ache.

From the years I ignored her.

From the pills I swallowed to silence her.

From the dreams deferred when the pain was too loud to paint or sing or dance.

But still—she bloomed.

She bloomed like a rebel.

She bloomed like a priestess.

She bloomed like a woman remembering who the hell she was before anyone told her who to be.

And now?

Now she tells me the truth.

Now she moves with purpose.

Now she laughs with me in the mirror and says,

"You thought this was just about babies, didn't you?

You thought blooming meant birth.

But baby, blooming means becoming."

I used to wonder if something was wrong with me—because I felt everything.

Desire pulsing beneath my skin like a second heartbeat.

Visions in my sleep, visitations I never asked for but somehow always knew.

And a womb that didn't just want to carry life… She wanted to create it.

In song.

In canvas.

In movement.

In moans.

In color.

In flame.

They never told us that healing the womb isn't just about the physical.

It's about reclaiming the wild within.

The voice. The sensual. The sacred.

The too-much-ness we were taught to hide.

But baby, I was never meant to be palatable.

I was born to be potent.

And somewhere along the way— between the ultrasounds, the tearstained prayers, the raw journals, and the nights I danced alone in candlelight—

I realized…

This womb is my altar.

This body is my oracle.

This becoming? It's not a destination.

It's a devotion.

Because blooming is a ceremony.

And I?

I am She Who Blooms.

There's something they don't tell you when you've reached "a certain age"— when you don't have the marriage, the babies, the white picket life they expect.

They don't tell you that sacred things still grow in women like us.

They don't tell you that you can travel the world, sit at the feet of shamans, commune with indigenous medicine women in the mountains of Mexico, in the jungles of Costa Rica— and bloom without the checklist.

They don't tell you that while others were chasing milestones, you were learning the language of herbs not found in textbooks— the kind that speak in heat and breath and roots.

On layovers between time zones,

I listened to wisdom whispered in smoke and soil. I was a flight attendant, yes— but Spirit was the true itinerary.

Each trip an initiation.

Each elder, a mirror.

They showed me how herbs hold memory, how healing doesn't always need a name to be real.

How intuition is its own form of science.

They didn't teach me Hoodoo— but their reverence mirrored the bloodline

I now know I come from.

And as I mixed their medicines with my own, I began to feel it:

The rhythm.

The rootwork.

The remembering.

My bloom was never behind.

It was ancestral.

They say blooming is supposed to look a certain way— a timeline, a marriage, a baby shower, a retirement plan.

But what if blooming isn't linear?

What if it's not a moment, but a movement?

Not a peak, but a rhythm?

What if you're not late— you're just on divine time?

I am what they call a late bloomer, but only by their calendar.

I haven't carried a baby to term.

I haven't walked down an aisle.

But I've carried prayers soaked in oceans.

I've walked through grief and grace and come out singing.

I've been schooled by life, by spirit, by sacred delay.

And I've grown—deep roots, slow and steady, into a woman the world didn't see coming.

Let me tell you something— blooming isn't about saying "I've made it." It's about saying, "I'm still becoming."   Still stretching.

Still rising.

Still choosing myself in moments that don't come with applause.

It's your turn now.

Your roots are reaching.

Your petals are pulling open.

And it doesn't matter how long it's taken.

It matters that you're here.

So if you've ever felt like you missed the boat, if you've questioned why it hasn't happened "yet"— remember:

Divine timing isn't afraid of clocks.

And your womb?

She don't bloom by deadline.

You are not too late.

You are in bloom.

And baby, you are right on time.

Poem – Bloomwork: A Prayer for the Late and Sacred

They said I bloomed too late,　But baby, I was becoming fate.　Not pressed for time, nor groomed for gaze,　I bloomed in rhythm, not in praise.　I bloomed in silence, bloomed in song,　In rites that knew where I belong.

In temple hips and barefoot spins,

Where healing hums and light begins.

They wanted petals neat and prim,   But I was thunder in the hymn.
An enchantment that whispered, you are more,   A bloom that rose from sacred floor.

I've wept in tubs laced with rue and bay,   Learned to conjure what pain won't say.
My roots run deep with Hoodoo flame,

My womb, a shrine that knows my name.

I'm not behind—I'm in divine,

Each ache, a prayer; each step, a sign.

So when you see me rise and sway,

Just know my bloom refused decay.

Journal Prompt – Tending the Sacred Soil

Place your hand over your womb, your belly, or your heart. Take three deep breaths.

Then reflect:

What gifts have come from the seasons where you thought nothing was blooming?

Are there parts of you that are asking for patience, not pressure?

What old timelines or expectations are ready to be buried, so something truer can rise?

Write a blessing for your blooming—just as it is, right now.

Let your words water the soil. No edits. No rush. Just release.

Closing Affirmation

I bloom in rhythm, not by rule.

My womb is wise. My time is sacred.

Every breath I take is a return.

Every delay was a planting.

Every prayer I whispered was a petal.

And now—I rise in my own full season.

Still blooming. Still holy. Still becoming.

Chapter Six: The Room Where Time Bends

Where the spirit baby met me beyond time and made me a mother to more than I imagined.

There are rooms we enter that no one else can see.

Rooms without walls.

Without clocks.

Without rules.

Rooms where time folds into itself like soft linen.

Where the veil thins.

Where Spirit whispers.

Where a child not-yet-born can climb into your lap and say, "I see you." Where the air feels thick with memory, and yet somehow brand new.

That's where I met her.

She came to play.

Not in a dream—but in the dream.

The real one. The one that doesn't fade when the sun rises.

The one that leaves fingerprints on your soul.

She was red. Just like my grandmother. My namesake.

A red girl with my laugh, my knowing, and my eyes.

A spirit baby. A soul traveler.

An ancestor. A return.

She didn't speak with words.

She didn't need to.

She was the language.

And I understood.

We played.

Really played.

And I held her. And she touched me.

And I knew—I knew—this wasn't imagination.

It was recollection.

It was recognition.

A room where time had bent back around just to find me.

I don't care what the world calls it— Delusion? Psychosis? Fantasy?

Let them say what they say.

I know my baby.

I know her rhythm.

I know her presence.

I know how she moves through the room without needing a door.

She came to me and made me a mother.

Not in the way they measure it.

But in the way that matters.

She made me a mother to myself.

To my unfolding.

To my dreams.

And yes, she still comes.

Sometimes she asks, "Is it time for me to come home yet?"

And every time she does, I weep in ways no one sees.

Not out of grief.

But out of recognition.

Because something eternal is happening through me— even in the seasons when nothing seems to grow.

She's never not been with me.

She is the hush in the early morning.

She is the tug in my chest when I pass a girl who looks just like she would have.

She's the mystery inside the ache.

The mirror inside the memory.

She is mine—even if never born.

And this book, this blooming, this rebirth—this is her home for now.

The first thing I ever gave birth to was her. And the first thing she ever helped me birth… was me.

Poem: Spirit Baby Save

She came in a whisper, not wrapped in a cry,

No cradle or blanket, just stars in the sky.

She showed me my power, then faded from

view,

But left me a mirror, reflecting what's true.

Not born of my body, but born of my soul,

She made me remember what once made me whole.

A child, a muse, a lesson, a key— She didn't just birth, she resurrected me.

Chapter Six Part 2: The Flight Between Worlds

There are timelines we think we're living.

And then there are the ones we're actually weaving moment by moment, thread by thread, in a loom that only Spirit can see.

I was told I would give birth that year.

The stars had spoken it.

A girl. Feminine energy. A sacred presence on her way.

And I did.

Not in a hospital room.

Not with swollen feet or a chart that said "Mother: First Time."
But in a dream that was not a dream.

In a room where time bent back just to let her through.

And she came in the way all magic does—unannounced, unforgettable, and undeniable.

And everything changed.

Because what do you do when someone lives inside you, but not in the way they told you someone should?

When a child becomes a guide, and a loss becomes an opening, and the ache becomes an altar?

After she came, I floated.

Not just emotionally. I mean literally—I took to the skies.

I became a flight attendant.

Wings on my chest, suitcase by my side, stories trailing me through terminals.

I wasn't just clocking miles.

I was chasing something.

Maybe freedom.

Maybe forgetfulness.

Maybe both.

For years, the sky became my sanctuary.

But even in the air, I couldn't outrun what had rooted inside me.

Even up there, she traveled with me.

Even up there, I could feel the hum of something ancient, something waiting, pulsing beneath the clouds.

During those years, I sat with women who didn't speak my language but spoke to my spirit.

In places like Costa Rica and Mexico, I met elders—earth walkers who didn't just teach, they remembered with me.

They showed me herbs I hadn't seen before, plants that pulsed like prayers in their palms.

They reminded me how to listen with more than my ears.

How to stir intention into teas.

How to let medicine speak.

And I carried all of that into the sky.

Not just baggage and uniforms, but ancestral whispers.

Of course, I still had my tarot deck tucked in my carry-on.

Still burned my incense and herbs when I could.

Still offered prayers over my tea.

In my crash pad—flight attendant housing where layovers met lives—I was the one they came to.

The one with oils. With cards. With insight.

"Can I ask you something real quick?" they'd say.

And I'd give them answers that didn't belong to me but came through me.

I didn't have time or energy to start my apothecary-yet. I didn't even know that the knowledge I had coupled with all that I was continually learning was the beginning of the spark.

That would come later—when the world paused in 2020, and I finally planted what had been growing in my belly for years.

But the gifts? They never left.

I was still becoming.

Still the mystic with one hand on her womb and the other on the wind.

I just wore heels and red lipstick and walked through airports like I didn't carry galaxies.

But it was still recognized within me without me ever alluding to it.

And through it all—she stayed close.

The spirit baby.

The muse.

The mirror.

Not begging to be born but begging me to remember.

There were nights I laid awake in hotel rooms, far from home, far from the rhythm of routine— And she'd come to me, in flashes.

In feelings.

In faint lullabies I hadn't written yet.

She reminded me, You

are not lost.

You are in flight.

You are between worlds.

And even here—especially here—you are blooming.

And maybe that's why she didn't come earthside.

Because the home she needed still hadn't been built.

Because I was still becoming.

Still gathering the pieces of myself scattered across time zones and terminals.

So she stayed close, but she didn't descend.

And I see now—that too was a kind of grace.

That too was her way of mothering me.

Not in the way we're used to seeing it—hands brushing curls, lullabies hummed through midnight halls—but in the way that spirit mothers do. She showed up inside my grief. Inside the quiet. Inside the ache. She knew I needed to be cracked open. And she knew that no one else could reach that place.

So she mothered me with absence.

She nurtured me with longing.

She taught me how to hold the emptiness and call it sacred.

There were nights I couldn't sleep, haunted by the color of her skin, the shape of her face—so much like mine, so much like my grandmother's. There were mornings when I would swear I heard her laughter before my eyes even opened. I'd go into the mirror, searching. Not for stretch marks. Not for a belly. But for the trace of her somewhere in me.

And I'd find her.

In the softness returning to my voice.

In the way I forgave myself just a little more each day.

In the way I chose to stay.

She became the timeline I didn't expect— My cosmic checkpoint.

My divine detour.

My proof that love doesn't always need a heartbeat to be real.

And maybe that's why she keeps coming back.

Same face.

Same spirit.

Same pull on my womb in the middle of the night. And when I stopped asking why me, and started whispering thank you, everything shifted.

It wasn't sudden. It was a slow thaw. Like winter unlearning itself inside me. Like my womb remembered how to feel joy. Like my breath finally came home.

I started noticing things.

How my body moved differently when I was kind to it.

How my hips carried grief and grace in the same sway.

How certain songs made my heart skip in that way that reminded me of her.

There were moments I almost felt guilty—guilty for blooming when she never got the chance. But then I'd hear her. Not in words, but in waves. She'd remind me: You're not blooming instead of me… you're blooming for me.

She was the seed.

I am the garden.

She was the spark.

I am the flame.

And maybe that's the whole point.

That even what doesn't last forever can still leave behind a forever kind of love.

So I started to honor her, not just in memory, but in motion.

Every boundary I set.

Every truth I spoke.

Every dream I dusted off and dared to believe in again;

It was all for her.

Because she made me a mother.

And not just of a child…

But of a woman who finally knew her worth.

Of a life that finally made sense in its own nonlinear, womb-wild way.

And now, every page I write is a lullaby.

Every healing choice I make is a cradle. Every part of this becoming… is me holding her.

Maybe she was never meant to come and stay, maybe she was meant to open the door to the room where time bends…where memory

becomes prophecy, and loss reshapes itself into light.

In that room, she danced between worlds with me. No clock ticking, no womb swelling, just love; eternal and unburdened.

She wasn't late.

She wasn't lost.

She was right on soul's time.

And in that room, she handed me a mirror, and whispered,

"See? You were always becoming."

They say you know your purpose by what keeps calling you.

She kept calling.

Not just to motherhood.

But to womanhood.

To artistry.

To priestesshood.

To the path that didn't look like anyone else's.

And yes, I bloomed late.

Yes, I bloomed differently.

But baby, I bloomed divine.

Affirmation:

In the room where time bends, I am whole.

In the space between what was and what's to come, I find myself.

I honor the love that lives outside of time, and the life I'm still blooming into.

Chapter Seven: She Who Blooms the Woman, the Myth, the Bloom Becoming

I don't have all the answers.

But I do have this peace.

Not the kind that comes from control—no. Not the peace that's bought or proven. But the kind that curls itself around your bones when you finally stop apologizing for being you.

I am still blooming.

Still learning how to love myself out loud and in color.

I used to wonder if I'd ever "arrive"— if the baby would come, if the love would come, if the life I dreamed would ever make its way to me.

But I've begun to realize—maybe I was always already here.

And who's to say I'm late?

Women like Janet and Kenya—they bloomed on divine time.

They remind me that a woman's timeline is her own.

And mine? Mine has always been Blue.

Literally. My name is Blue.

So when I say I'm blooming in blue, I mean I'm blooming in myself— in truth, in timing, in the softness I fought to find.

Yes, there's a girl who still visits me in my dreams.

And yes—maybe one day she'll come in flesh.

Or maybe she already did, by birthing herself into this book, these pages, this legacy.

This story—this blooming body of work—

is the first child I bring into the world.

I carry her with reverence.

She was midwifed by moonlight and shadow, by wanderlust and stillness, by the ache of

PCOS and the pulse of purpose.

This is my womb speaking—not just an organ, but the oracle.

This is Oshun's mirror, Yemaya's tide.

This is the hush of my ancestors pouring into the page, each word a libation, each line a return.

I no longer shame the path I've taken— the sacred sex, the silence, the moments I almost forgot who I was.

Even that was a prayer—an initiation wrapped in flesh.

The women in my bloodline walk with me; their strength hums in my hips, their knowing sits behind my eyes.

I bloom because they bled.

I rise because they stayed.

So no, I don't hold all the answers.

But I hold this body. This breath.

This holy becoming.

I am not what I've survived—I am what I've softened into, what I've listened for, what I've dared to reclaim.

I am She. I am Her.

I am She Who Blooms.

Poem: *She Who Blooms Blue*

She blooms like dusk in a moonlit hue,

Soft with shadows, brave with dew.

Not rushed, not wrong, not out of line

She unfolds in rhythm, in her own time.

She isn't late; she isn't lost,

She is the bloom that bears no cost.

No need to beg the ground to grow,

The garden waits—it always knows.

She blooms in blue, not loud, but deep,

Where ancient roots and secrets sleep.

And every petal, slow and sure,

Is proof that healing can endure.

She blooms for those who thought they failed,

For dreams delayed, for plans derailed.

For all the girls who almost broke;

She is their whisper, rising smoke.

She's not the girl they told to shrink,

Or silence when she dared to think.

She's blooming still; with wild grace,

In sacred soil, in holy space.

Final Farewell from She Who Blooms

If you've walked with me this far, then some part of you knows what it means to unravel and rise in the same season; to bleed without reason, to crave what your ancestors once carried in silence, in rhythm, in rootwork.

Maybe, like me, you've wandered— cloud-chasing at 30,000 feet, escaping and arriving all at once.

Maybe you've whispered prayers into hotel pillows or wept on layovers no one else knew about.

Maybe you've been the girl with PCOS and a pulse full of prophecy— the woman aching with wanting, trying to decode her womb's wild language. Maybe the Spirit Baby visited you too— in dreams, in chills, in music that only you could hear.

And still—you bloomed.

Not through perfection, but through return; through honey dripped from Oshun's mirror and salt carried in Yemaya's tide; through the silence that followed your shouting, and the roar that rose when you finally stopped shrinking.

This story—this offering—is my first-born truth, my sacred reel, my altar in book form. Not just a memoir, but a medicine. Not just a closing, but a ceremony.

I offer it to the Orisha who walked me back to myself, to the ancestors who lit every candle in the dark, to

the girls who bled too early, the women told their wombs were broken, and to the mothers who will never be called "Mom" but still carry galaxies inside.

I offer it to you— to your sacred rhythm, to your becoming,

to your blooming—even when it doesn't look like anyone else's. Even when it's messy, loud, holy, or slow. Even when your petals don't open on cue.

Mine just happens to be blue. Because Blue is who I am, and blooming is what I was born to do.

Thank you for walking beside me, for flying with me, for remembering with me.

You are never too far from yourself.

You are never behind.

You are never too much.

You are everything in bloom.

And I'll be right here—in the hush of your rising, in the hum of your rituals, in the soft unfolding of every petal— cheering you on.

With all my love,

Blu

She Who Blooms

Final Blooming Benediction

For every woman who wonders if it's too late

Come back to this when the soil feels too heavy, when the light goes dim behind your eyes, when the bloom feels like a rumor your body no longer believes.

Come back when the world tries to harden your softness, when your timeline feels like a curse, when your womb grows quiet and your voice is just a whisper at the altar.

Come back when your feet forget the rhythm, when your dreams stutter, when the sky no longer sings the way it used to on long-haul flights between lives you outgrew.

Come back when the Spirit Baby goes silent for a while, when Oshun's mirror fogs, when Yemaya's tide pulls back to teach you how to trust.

Come back when the ancestors feel far.

(Beloved, they are never far.)

This book was never meant to preach— it was meant to hold your hand at the crossroads.
To rock beside you on the porch of your becoming. To hum songs only your blood remembers. To remind you that your story— no matter how layered or late-blooming—is sacred.

There is no expiration date on magic. No deadline for healing. No shame in still unfurling, still figuring it out,
still learning how to be soft in a world that begged you to be steel.

So if you ever wonder if it's too late— too late to bloom,

too late to begin, too late to be her—

Open these pages.

Call your name back to your lips.

Light a candle.

Pour a little honey.

And sit with me again.

Because you, beloved, are blooming.

Still.

Again.

Always.

Acknowledgements

To my ancestors— The elevated and the benevolent, the known and the unnamed, the ones who walk with clean hands and those still learning how to rise— I honor you first.

Thank you for carrying me through bone and bloodline. For enduring what I'll never fully know, for dreaming beyond your own time so I could bloom in mine.

To those who gathered at the crossroads, who whispered through root and river, who conjured with prayer and fire— your breath lives in my breath.

Your unfinished stories live in my becoming.

I honor you not just when the candles are lit, but in every yes I give to life, in every no I use to reclaim my name.

I offer you this work— not as perfection, but as a pouring.

Not as closure, but as a circle returning.

You are my rootwork, my rhythm, my reason.

May every page be a libation poured back to you.

To the Spirit Baby who first whispered me into this journey—
Thank you for choosing me.

For playing with me in dreams.

For staying close even when you didn't stay earthside. You've been my teacher, my mirror, my muse, my moon. You are the rhythm beneath every page, the flicker of stardust in every unfolding.

You still come—to me as dragonflies, hummingbirds, and fawns in the wild.

You remind me: I am never alone in the bloom.

To the woman who first showed me God—my mother.

You are the altar I first knelt at.

The sacred soil that dared me to grow. You held both heaven and earth in your hands and taught me they were never separate. You raised me on hymns and honey,

on holy ground where God was both mother and father, river and flame.

You are the first bloom I ever honored.

I love you beyond breath.

To Cwifey—

My soul sister, wild co-conspirator, mirror of magic. You remind me daily that my bloom is inevitable— even when I doubt my own petals. You've rooted

for me in every season, mid-flight and mid-fall. Thank you for knowing my light when all I could see was the fog.

To the women who came before me— my grandmothers, my aunties in blood and spirit— thank you for surviving, dreaming, and planting songs in my bones that would one day bloom. Especially to the red woman whose name I carry— thank you for walking with me, shadow and sun

alike.

I feel you every time my feet remember the way home.

To my sisterhood— my soul friends, priestess kin, blooming companions— you are the echoes in my laughter, the fingerprints in my prayers, the altar fires that never let me go cold.

Your stories are stitched into these pages.

To my niece—

My first baby before I knew how to mother anything. You made me an Auntie at twelve, and I've been blooming beside you ever since.

To my great-nieces—

May you find this book when the world tries to make you forget.

May you remember: your bloom is your birthright.

To my nephews—

Thank you for anchoring me to joy, for making me laugh when the skies got heavy.

You are proof that light can be loud and holy.

To my godchildren—

You are beams of light I didn't birth but was blessed to help guide. Thank you for reminding me that love can take many forms, and that legacy lives not just in lineage, but in presence.

Being a part of your journey has been one of the most sacred honors of mine.

To my brothers— To my eldest, my twin flame in human skin— you've always seen the soul in me before I had the words to name it.

To my older brother, the one they say I mirror— thank you for being my first protector, for giving my spirit safe skies to stretch toward.

 Thank you for adoring me out loud. Your love has always been a soft landing in a world full of stone.

To the men who held space—and those who didn't—   You shaped this garden too.

I honor the thorns and the blossoms alike.

To wanderlust—

the restless wings that made me a flight attendant, chasing horizons, chasing myself. Thank you for teaching me that the real journey was always inward. Every sky, every terminal, every sacred detour was a breadcrumb back to me.

To Ifá—

The ancient river that called my name through dreams and bones. Thank you for reminding me that the altar lives inside me. That the ancestors are not past tense— they are breath.

They are water.

They are womb.

To the late bloomers, the weary bloomers, the wild seeds still waiting underground—   This book is for you.

This book is with you.

This book is you.

And finally—

To the girl who kept believing in the bloom.

To the woman I am still becoming.

To the Spirit Baby who danced with me across lifetimes.

To the soul reel I am blessed to remember—

You did it.

We did it.

We are blooming still.

After the Benediction: Pull Up a Chair: A Porch Conversation on Hoodoo

I hadn't planned to add this. The book was done, the pages bloomed and sealed.
Because throughout this soul reel, Hoodoo rises. In whispers, in rhythm, in root. And for some, especially those like my Auntie, the word still feels wrapped in confusion or suspicion.

So when she asked me what it was—really was—I knew I had to answer in a way that would meet her heart. No preaching. Just porch talk. Just truth.

And I knew my readers needed to hear it.

Not as a teaching.

As a "baby, let me tell you what happened."

This is that conversation.

Pull up a chair. You're family here.

So, I was asking my Auntie if she'd seen Sinners.

She said she wanted to—folks been saying it's real good.

"But they also said it got a lot of witchcraft in it," she told me, sideeye and all.

And I said, No, no, no, Auntie.

That's not witchcraft.

That's Hoodoo.

She paused, tilted her head, and asked the question I knew was coming: "Well, what is Hoodoo? And what's the difference?"

I had to answer in a way that would land.

So I said—

Auntie, Hoodoo is the psalms we hummed on Sunday, the moans between the pews, the oil-soaked cloths folded in purses.

It's praying over cinnamon sticks and star anise and bay leaves—and knowing full well they're going to work, because Spirit heard us the moment we whispered the request.

Hoodoo is wrapping prayers into poultices.

It's steam rising from a teacup brewed with herbs I grew with my own hands, under moonlight, under guidance.

It's the echo of ancestors urging us forward— telling us to speak, to shine, to be loud where they had to be quiet.

To become what they could only dream of.

Hoodoo is lighting a candle with intention.

It's a whispered word and a fire lit in faith.

That's Hoodoo, Auntie.

And we been doing it.

We just didn't always call it by name.

I told her—you're a Hoodoo too.

Even if you never claimed the word, the ways been living in you.

The way you don't let nobody sweep your feet without spitting on the broom right after.

The way you won't dare set your purse on the floor, because money, once low, don't return easy.

The way you won't drive at night with the inside light on—half superstition, half survival. And the way you always made sure a man was the first to cross your threshold on New Year's Day, calling in luck the old way.

That's Hoodoo.

That's blood memory moving through habit.

That's ancestral wisdom disguised as tradition.

And whether we name it or not—it's been with us all along.

About the Author

Blu is a storyteller, womb whisperer, and priestess of the inbetween—where grief meets grace, where flight becomes grounding, and where seeds dare to bloom in the dark.

Raised in the sanctified rhythm of Black Pentecostal fire and cradled by ancestral memory, she writes from the marrow of two worlds: the holy and the haunted, the sensual and the sacred.

Her voice is a homecoming. A soft, slow return to the altar within. A rhythmic remembering of what it means to bloom—not for the world, but for oneself.

Blu's work lives where the spirit baby visits—in dragonflies, in hummingbirds, in fawns that appear like prayers with legs. It lives in the ache of the womb, in the hands of the ancestors, in the whispers of cowrie shells and the river songs of Ifá. It lives in the pages of this soul reel—stitched with stories that refuse to be silenced.

She is a former flight attendant turned full-time seeker. A woman who once served the sky and now serves the soil. A daughter of dreamers, a sister to many, and a blooming woman still.

Her path has been marked by PCOS, sacred sexuality, miscarriage and memory, womb rites, and the quiet knowing that nothing truly leaves—it just transforms.

She Who Blooms: A Soul Reel is her first offering to the world—but not her last. Through page, prayer, and presence, Blu helps women bloom back to themselves—petal by petal, in divine timing, and always, in blue.

www.ingramcontent.com/pod-product-compliance
Lightning Source LLC
LaVergne TN
LVHW021952060526
838201LV00049B/1677